Also from GHF Press
Making the Choice
When Typical School Doesn't Fit Your Atypical Child

— *Forging Paths*
Beyond Traditional Schooling

If This is a Gift, Can I Send it Back?
Surviving in the Land of the Gifted and Twice Exceptional

— *Learning in the 21st Century*
How to Connect, Collaborate, and Create

— *How to Work and Homeschool*
Practical Tips, Advice, and Strategies from Parents

Educating Your Gifted Child
How One Public School Teacher Embraced Homeschooling

— *Self-Directed Learning*
Documentation and Life Stories

✓ *Gifted, Bullied, Resilient*
A Brief Guide for Smart Families

Writing Your Own Script
A Parent's Role in the Gifted Child's Social Development

Coming Soon from GHF Press
www.giftedhomeschoolers.org/ghf-press/

Bob Yamtich
Effective Communication for Gifted and 2e Kids

Paula Prober
Your Rainforest Mind

Kelly Hirt
Twelve Ways to Lift Up Our Twice-Exceptional Children

Amy Harrington
Radical Unschooling

Kathleen Humble
Gifted Myths

Lori Dunlap
A Guide for College Admissions Professionals

Micro-Schools:

Creating Personalized Learning on a Budget

By Jade Rivera

Edited by Sarah J. Wilson

Published by GHF Press
A Division of Gifted Homeschoolers Forum
3701 Pacific Ave. SE - PMB #609
Olympia, WA 98501

ISBN-13: 978-0692609095 (GHF Press)
ISBN-10: 0692609091

Cover design by Shawn Keehne
www.shawnkeehne.com • skeehne@mac.com

Dedication

To my past, present, and future students.

Contents

Acknowledgments

First, I would like to thank my husband for his love, support, and devotion. My dear friends Marielle Cammarata and Sara Yamtich for their sustained attention, advice, and input on every angle of this book. There are not enough thank yous in the world for Bob Yamtich. You have been my collaborator and good buddy from day one of this micro-school adventure. Your perspective and hilarious insights have kept me going, even when I thought I had nowhere to go.

I would also like to thank (in no particular order) Dr. Linda Silverman, Pamela Price, Jen Merrill, Paula Prober, Dr. Melanie Hayes, Anne Beneventi, Shanna Philipson, and Nicole Linn for their encouragement and advice.

Thank you Corin Barsily Goodwin and Sarah Wilson for taking a chance on me and letting me write this book for GHF Press.

Last, I do not know what I would do without the support of my online friends, the GHF Bloggers, and the members of my private support group, The Gifted Family. I was once a lonely blogger and educator, you took me in, helped me get clear in my vision, feel my value, and gave me a home.

Thank you.

Introduction

Take a moment to reflect on your own education. Most of the readers of this book will have spent their youth learning in the traditional manner, like I did, inside brick-and-mortar schools with teachers, rows of desks, grades, and honor roll.

You may have gotten the sense that your school was a factory, concerned with output, manageability, and efficiency above all else. You were correct. Interestingly, the public at large is mostly unaware of the dubious origins of modern schooling practices.

In his essay, *The Prussian-Industrial History of Public Schooling*, Yehudi Meshchaninov clearly and concisely explains exactly how and why Horace Mann, the "Father of Common Schooling," adopted this method of educating young people:

> *This is the legacy of the Prussian model. Designed to ensure control, it systematically disempowers students and adults alike with ruthless efficiency. Infantilized and fearful, its members are left weak—conditioned to obey those in command. It was this system that Horace Mann transplanted to U.S. shores in 1843.*[1]

No talking.
No running.
No fidgeting.

What was your experience? Did you answer the instructor's questions? Or did you ask the questions yourself? Every time you raised your hand, did you receive a subtle eye-roll and exasperated sigh in response? Were you mucking up your teacher's attempts to communicate a plan in a finite amount of time? Was your name constantly written on the board for visiting, talking out of turn, and generally creating complications?

How were you punished for these transgressions? Was your recess taken away? Were you isolated from the other children? Made to sit in the hall? Maybe you internalized all of these messages and started to think, "Maybe I *am* bad or stupid. What is *wrong* with me?"

Is it sucking the life out of you to watch your child or your students endure the same, possibly worse, treatment?

When you talk to other adults about your frustration with traditional school, what do they say in response?

"Well, we turned out fine."

"If it was good enough for us, then it's good enough for them."

Or, my personal favorite, "Life is hard. You spend a lot of time doing things you don't want to do. It's better that they learn that early."

In 2014, I went to see Alfie Kohn, a proponent of progressive education, speak in San Francisco, and I asked him how he would respond to these types of questions. He looked at me and queried, "*Are we fine?*"

Based on what I see and experience, no. No, we are not. More than ever, people are expressing concern over adolescent mental health, and while mental health issues are caused by a constellation of factors, it is known that environment plays a part. According to a 2013 report put out by the Centers for Disease Control and Prevention, it is estimated that, in a given year, 13 to 20 percent of children living in the United States—up to one out of five children—experience a mental disorder such as attention-deficit/hyperactivity disorder, anxiety, or depression, and the number of children with a mental disorder increases with age. Based on the conversations I have had with parents, some children are medicated as a first line of defense. Additionally, schools are forced to worry more about standardized test scores than actually serving the needs of the children taking those tests.[2]

Gifted children develop asynchronously, and a gifted child with a learning disability is considered twice-exceptional (2e).[3,4] Myths and lies about gifted and 2e children continue:

- All children are gifted.

- They'll be fine on their own.

- She isn't achieving the way a gifted child should.

Perhaps you are a teacher who is fed up with the inequity and bureaucracy of traditional school.

Maybe you are a teacher whose own child is gifted or twice-exceptional and still you cannot seem to get him the services he deserves.

Maybe you are a parent who refuses to sit through another IEP meeting knowing you will be disappointed by the lack of follow-through in services for your child.

Maybe you sent your child to private school only to be shocked to discover the problem became even worse when you ponied upwards of $20,000 a year for your child to sit in the office and not be invited to birthday parties.

Maybe you have picked a career and sacrificed to make it work. You are successful but unfulfilled—doing what you should do, rather than what you want to do. Every morning that you wake up for work, you feel like you are stuck in a "swamp of sadness" and you cannot remember the last time you felt hopeful. When you hear Queen's 'I've Got to Break Free on the radio, you weep. (All right, maybe that was just me). Regardless, it is time for you to make a revolutionary change in your life.

If you have come to this book, it means you are done compromising your values. *You are ready to make a change.*

At the heart of this book lies a simple but potent message: *People cannot be standardized, and neither can their education.*

Starting or enrolling in a micro-school is not like homeschooling. It is not a co-op. Nor is it like traditional public school or private school. It is education on the cutting edge. It will be unlike any educational experience you have ever had. It is hard to be a trailblazer, but necessity breeds innovation. This book is perhaps the first road map for grassroots micro-schooling.

My hope in writing this is that you will feel empowered to take control of the education in your gifted and twice-exceptional (2e) community. I want you to read this book and then go find more families like yours who are sick of the fixed mindset under which too many traditional schools operate. Find more people like you who can see that progressive education is the lifeline of positive social change.

If you decide to move forward with your own micro-school, you will sacrifice. Perhaps you will cry. And maybe you will just sit there numb, immobilized by stress. Perhaps you already experience this and feel pretty ineffective. Imagine if you redirected those emotional and organizational efforts toward something that you can control. The stress will not go away completely, but the hopelessness will.

OK. Let's do this.

Chapter One
How I Got Here

Few people intentionally put themselves on the path to teach gifted children. They may want to teach smart, high-achieving children, but that is an extremely narrow view of giftedness. Teaching programs rarely cover the reality of what gifted children need, which turns out to be quite a bit different than what is provided to the majority of school-age children. Teaching highly sensitive, quirky, socially challenged children is a profession many people are thrust into by circumstance. I was pushed into alternative education for gifted children by revelations about my own educational experience. Others are pulled in by the realization that the traditional system is failing their child. What follows is my personal journey into alternative education.

In high school, I grasped complex scientific concepts with relative ease, but I didn't show any real talent in math. In fact, I had been a straight C student in math since the third grade. And honestly, I had even less talent for memorization. Although never formally diagnosed, I find that I have a lot in common with my dyslexic students. I believed that because I was not good in math and memorization, something was wrong with me.

Then there was the unfortunate aspect of my home life. In an autobiographical blog post I wrote I described my childhood this way:

Growing up there were drugs, there was desperation, and there was poverty.

Most of our (my little brother's, little sister's, and my) lives with my mother and stepfathers was spent moving from state to state. At first we moved for the military, next from poverty, and then from the law. At best, I was neglected. At worst, I endured bouts of the kind of attention that should have sent my parents to jail. Somewhere along the line, I was diagnosed as gifted. I would hop from gifted program to gifted program in the public schools. I received fragments of an education by teachers who openly labeled me as "too sensitive" and "intense." I was (and probably still am on a few levels) a creative, divergent, gifted mess.

One of my earliest education-related nightmares occurred the day I came to school and realized that everyone had learned long division the day before. I had been absent, recovering from a long few days and nights of refereeing for my parents. I walked up to my teacher's desk to ask for an explanation and was immediately barked at to sit down. I quickly grabbed the pass and ran to the bathroom to sit in a stall and shame spiral, alone. The tears rolled down my face as I stared into the fluorescent bathroom lights and envisioned the path of loserdom that surely awaited me. I returned to class, unnoticed, red faced, and snotty. I sat in my chair and stared at my neighbor's paper as he solved problem after problem. He told me, "Hey! Stop cheating!" I said, "I'm not cheating, I'm figuring it out." I'll never understand the refusal of my teacher to teach me. Was it because I was gifted? Poor? Brown? [5]

My favorite teacher in high school was my creative writing teacher, Sarah Applegate, who urged me to apply to The Evergreen State College. Luckily, I was accepted, because it was the only college I applied to.

At Evergreen I was not forced into prerequisites, so I could shop around and find the disciplines that truly spoke to my heart. I landed in a course named "Introduction to Natural Sciences." We learned in teams and all of our work was tied to real world issues such as climate change and nutrition. In this collaborative environment, every kind of talent was needed and valued. I felt like I had a purpose. It did not matter that I was not great at arithmetic because I became good at math, the real kind of math that is used to solve actual problems. I remember it felt like my consciousness was expanding at the speed of light. I had found my educational fit.

Straight out of college, I was awarded a Fulbright scholarship for chemistry research in Thailand. While in Thailand, I read a Harper's article that changed my life, although it was impossible to know the extent of the impact at the time. The article was titled, "Against School: How Public Education Cripples our Kids and Why," by John Taylor Gatto, a former New York State and New York Teacher of the Year. Gatto outlined in detail, with historical evidence, exactly how our schools are designed to keep people obedient and unquestioning:

> [W]e must wake up to what our schools really are: laboratories of experimentation on young minds, drill centers for the habits and attitudes that corporate society demands. Mandatory education serves children only incidentally; its real purpose is to turn them into servants.[6]

Upon my return from Thailand to Washington state, I took a position as a Title One reading assistant in a local elementary school. My job was to work with small groups of struggling readers to help them bring their reading skills up to grade level. Teaching children to read is still a huge point of pride for me. I should have known right then that my future was in education, but the guilt of not putting my chemistry degree to work was nagging at me. I foolishly thought that if I did not work as a chemist, my time in college was a waste—a typical freshly graduated, early twenties mindset.

I went to work as a food chemist, then a lab manager at a small community college, and finally ended up in the San Francisco Bay Area as a research and development chemist.

Throughout my career as a chemist, I was met with unnecessary competitiveness, other people's power issues, and a deep disregard for interpersonal connection. Through gentle probing of my science colleagues, I learned that the people contributing to our unhealthy workplace had learned to approach their work this way in school. I found this environment stifled innovation and creativity—two of my most cherished values. So I quit.

I had always been pretty good with kids. Upon moving to the Bay Area, I made a friend who worked as a nanny while she studied for her master's degree. She did quite well and seemed to have a lot of fun. In desperate need of fun and a job, I put out an online ad. In a short matter of time, it became known that if you had clever children who liked science and art, I was the nanny to hire.

One family I worked for homeschooled three gifted girls. These spirited young ladies would often attend group classes at a small progressive school for the gifted. The moment I heard of the school I was brimming with questions. What is a progressive school? What does it mean to be gifted? The mother of the three girls casually mentioned that I should visit the school and see if they would like me to lead some chemistry classes. I was knocking on their door the next day.

Shortly after my hire as the chemistry teacher, I was brought on as a full-time mentor. I had a lot of baggage to unpack about what it looked like to work hard, pay attention, and show respect. My first bump in the road occurred when I saw two students viewing a website other than the one I had instructed my students to look at. We were learning about Fibonacci sequences in nature. All I could see was that they were not doing what I had asked, when what they had actually done was take a moment to research the mathematician's biography. After a tearful meeting (for them) and an embarrassing meeting (for me), I realized I was going to have to radically shift my paradigm if I was going to have any success working with these students.

I facilitated the class of younger children as they learned independently and as a group. I taught chemistry and general science to the rest of the school. I developed a curriculum that was completely project-based, with full choice given to the students. They loved it. It was then I knew that I was doing my life's work. Many people remarked that I seem to have an intuitive sense of how an alternative program should work. Honestly, I was just teaching the way I wished I had been taught, a lot like the way I was taught at Evergreen. I was by no means perfect at it. But I cared, I researched, and I tried.

It was at this time my close friend and colleague, Bob Yamtich, introduced me to Non-Violent Communication, which quickly became my preferred communication strategy, not only in the classroom but in life. Soon, my students felt pride in their efforts and eagerly suggested cool new things they wanted to learn. Best of all, they went home and told their parents, "I like school!" I began to understand that working in partnership with children, treating them with respect, and doing my best to make sure their needs were met could create a sturdy foundation for children to blossom into autonomous, joyful learners. This continues to inform my teaching philosophy and standards.

Unfortunately, after teaching there for two years, the school closed, but I was quickly offered the position of lead educator at another program. While that program was being organized, I taught out of a living room and a garage. It was common to joke about how I was one step away from teaching in a van down by the river. This took place over a year and it was then that I realized the heart of these schools was not a fancy facility or access to amazing technology, though those things are fun and help meet needs for comfort and ease, and I certainly would not turn them down. No, the heart of these programs is the families, the students, and the teachers all coming together to learn and play.

Once the next program was running, and despite not actually owning the business, I was immediately hit with the challenge of keeping the school's doors open, which included navigating complicated relationships and working to build and maintain enrollment—all while teaching essentially solo and trying to meet the educational needs of a diverse and intense population of families. I began to understand what it meant to run a school as a business and the deep complexities of interdependence that come along with that. Under this great strain, I held on as tight as I could to my teaching philosophies and prayed that something would give. Three years later, it did. The program ended, and I was left once again to find a new venue for my mission.

The program took such a toll on me that I considered giving up progressive education and taking up waitressing for a living. Thankfully, my waitressing fantasies were quickly quashed. I would have hated missing out on what came next. A group of families I had previously worked with recruited me, desperately wanting to create an appropriate learning environment for their children. Once again, innovation was born out of necessity.

Enter One Room Micro-School for Gifted and Twice-Exceptional Students. For the next two years, this program would be my baby. The buck stopped with me. I named the program One Room out of my love of the idea of a one-room schoolhouse (a familial and intimate place to learn, but without the corporal punishment and rote memorization, of course).

We started in a donated space in the upstairs room of a musical theater and dance school for children, a business owned by one of my student's parents. I will be forever grateful to the families, as they pushed me professionally to become a better teacher, businesswoman, and overall person. This was the moment I began to take serious ownership of my philosophies and methods. A friend created a website for me, and I began blogging about my work. I felt stronger in my boots than ever before.

Over the years, I learned a lot about educating, administering, and working with families. Alongside my students, I learned who I am, what motivates me, and what I am capable of. I am proud to share my strategies and my philosophies with you.

Connection over Perfection

In this book, you will find detailed guidance on how to establish your own micro-school for gifted/2e children. In its simplest form, a micro-school is just a school that children may attend part-time or full-time. While I love the flexibility inherent in that format, we did so much more at One Room: We gave that same part-time option and provided an appropriate academic *and* social-emotional challenge. This included individualizing almost every expectation and request made of the learner. Sound impossible? Not when you make an effort to have a connected, compassionate relationship with each gifted learner (and family) you are serving. It is extremely challenging, but not impossible.

The ideal micro-school outlined in this book may look different to the reality-based micro-school your community is about to create. When the rubber meets the road, we are all just doing the best we can.

Over the years, I have taught in a wide variety of settings. My first experience took place in a huge house with its own pool. I have taught out of people's living rooms and garages, a small storefront next to a park, a small upstairs room of a children's musical theater business. I have had programs next to smelly restaurants and worked in spaces with fluorescent lights. I have taught all day, and then had to stay after to act as janitor when we did not have enough money to hire someone skilled to clean the facility. I have set up hot plates in lieu of a kitchen. I have worked in one giant echo-filled room where a quiet space was not to be found outside of the bathroom.

I have struggled with what to teach, how to teach, and whom to teach. I have fought back tears as I trashed student-requested activities that took days to plan after a student rolled his eyes and said, "Yeah, I'm not that into that anymore." Now I know better, but, dang, it was it tough back in the day.

When it comes down to it, the programs are not about the lessons, but about the community and giving children the chance to learn on their own terms.

Full disclosure: I have had the various elements of everything I outline here in one program or another, but not all at the same time. As you may already know, gifted people are notorious for letting *perfect* be the enemy of good or even great. Do not fall into this trap. Even when operating with fifty to sixty percent of what is in this book, I have witnessed deep healing and growth for everyone involved. I have had fun learning with my students, and they have had fun, too. Use this book as an empowering brainstorm of what might be possible, not as hard and fast rules.

Much to my amazement, on the whole, my students were still happier with me than in a traditional school. I can only credit this loyalty to my commitment to connection. The one constant that I had in every environment has been me. No matter what we did or did not have, my students always knew that their needs were equal to mine. It is important to me that my students know I have their backs.

A parent of one of my students (and dear friend, confidante, and supporter) put it this way:

> *Traditional school was a constantly shaken snow globe and they [my students] could never settle into themselves. You stopped the snow globe from shaking. Emotional needs never trump anything in traditional school. If you reflect [on the] industrialization of education, emotions are too variable (especially the extreme ones of those with overexcitablities) to be standardized, so they get ignored.*

Every accommodation you make, every chance to share power with a kid, will serve to enhance all of your lives.

Chapter Two
Why Micro-Schools for Gifted/2e Children?

You may be surprised to read that a majority of my students have been kicked out of pre-school. That's right, kicked out of *pre-school*. From their first experience of school, they received a powerful and damaging message: *You're not appreciated, you're not accepted, and we don't want you here.*

I hear two main reasons for my students being kicked out of preschool: 1) The overstimulation of group learning triggered aggressive behaviors, and 2) The children became disenchanted when they realized that other kids did not want to listen to half-hour-long lectures on astronomy or dinosaurs. My students gravitate toward subject matter beyond their years and show an aptitude for understanding and integrating knowledge in those subjects with a depth that can make a typical teacher feel uneasy. Sadly, most teachers are not taught how to relate to a child with a greater knowledge base about a subject than they have. And they certainly are not trained to empathize with the intensity and sensitivity that go hand in hand with that precociousness.

I have heard stories from parents of profoundly gifted children who are miserable in preschool because of their innate perfectionistic fear of not knowing what to do when. They may not know when and how to fold their sleeping mat, or they may be afraid of what will happen if they have dirty noses during nap time and do not have any tissues. This anxiety can also be the culprit behind these children derailing lesson plans and controlling group play.

Very few parents start out with a working knowledge of giftedness and twice-exceptionality. Particularly, first-time parents tend to think all children speak in full sentences at nine months or teach themselves to read at three, to name a couple of examples. It is not until problems arise in school that they begin to sense that their child is somehow different, and that realization sends them on a quest for information. You may have heard this quip somewhere: "A worried parent does better research than the FBI." This statement is not just clever, it is also very true.

Sooner or later (ideally sooner), they stumble across Dr. Linda Silverman's list of gifted characteristics,[7] and all of a sudden everything becomes clear. Below I offer an overview of many of these characteristics and why micro-schools for gifted and twice-exceptional children are well designed to meet the needs of these outlier students. In my experience, these traits are even more obvious in twice-exceptional children. The asynchrony found in gifted children is more pronounced in twice-exceptional children.[8]

Gifted children reason well (are good thinkers)

Gifted children give complicated, detailed explanations. They tend to expound on topics they feel passionate about, then feel dejected when their level of enthusiasm is not matched. We all experience a mismatched level of enthusiasm with another human on occasion. When the mismatch is a nearly daily occurrence, we can see why many gifted children begin to feel depressed in a traditional classroom stuck with age-mates, rather than intellectual peers.

A child who reasons well can see ambiguity in factual information. I see this all the time when it comes to assessing bias. Frequently, my students will take a look at what is presented as factual information and question the source of the material. They intuit that history is written by the victors and that the victor's best interest may be to not truthfully recount the details of a battle or power shift. They will question the fundamental laws of space and time as they relate to perception. Every lesson turns into a philosophical discussion.

In one of my favorite interviews, Richard Feynman, physicist and Nobel Laureate, shared his experience of learning algebra. Without instruction, he intuitively grasped that the idea was to solve for the variable, or x. It did not matter to him how he did that, what steps he took, or whether he showed his work. Luckily he had a family that understood and respected him. He was never made to feel inferior because he could not show his work. Unfortunately, many children are made to feel inferior, and the damage is lasting.

Moreover, given that many gifted children have highly developed needs for autonomy and control, the creation of a product designed solely to demonstrate learning can feel like a violation, especially if the product has specific requirements. They know what they know and see little need for demonstrating mastery for something as superficial as a grade or gold star. They crave individualized interaction with meaningful feedback that values their efforts and what they have created.

Gifted children learn rapidly

When a gifted child learns more quickly than the other children in her learning environment, she often finishes work or understands concepts in a fraction of the time the teacher has allotted. Then the child is tasked to sit still and wait, something gifted children do not necessarily do well. When not occupied, gifted children will try doodling, talking to their neighbor, and occasionally acting out (not surprisingly). They are bored and crave attention, but teachers are preoccupied helping others accomplish what the gifted child finished with no guidance. While she sits there with nothing to do, she is robbed of additional opportunities to learn, extend her knowledge, and pursue her own passions.

Gifted children have extensive vocabularies

An impressive vocabulary is one the easiest identifiers for gifted children. Unfortunately, it is also one of the easiest markers for bullies. (For an excellent discussion of giftedness and bullying, check out

Pamela Price's book, *Gifted, Bullied, Resilient: A Brief Guide for Smart Families*.) When a student talks differently or uses more advanced vocabulary than students his age, he becomes a target. A friend related a story to me about her son's difficult time at a local science meet-up. He had made a clever joke about Schrodinger's cat (a reference to a quantum mechanics experiment), which fell flat. His combination of prior knowledge and vocabulary led to blank stares, eye rolls, and responses of "What does that even mean?" and "Why are you so weird?" He had come to the meeting hopeful to find peers, but instead was quickly alienated.

The families I served in my programs have shared with me numerous stories of how their highly verbal children stuck out at school. Their children were taunted with sarcastic questions like "Why do you talk weird?" or "Don't you ever shut up?"

Too many experiences like this can trigger depression and anxiety which could take years to process, robbing children of the joy and health we wish for them.

Gifted children have excellent memories

I have heard stories of gifted children who accurately remember events from when they were still in the crib. They remember everything their parents have said, for better or worse. If these children are accurately remembering everything they read, then that makes repetitive lessons and "close reading" obsolete and an egregious waste of time. What is the gifted child supposed to do while the rest of the class is doing everything they can to recall facts that the gifted child memorized long ago?

Gifted children have a long attention span . . .

. . . when engaged! And that engagement needs to be deep and complex. These students need a lot of time with the subjects they love. Understanding their passions is vital to their self-actualization. In order to respect this aspect of a gifted child, lesson plans must be adjusted or compromised. I learned quickly that pushing my agenda when a child was otherwise engaged got me nowhere fast.

Gifted children tend to be intense, highly sensitive, and energetic

These characteristics come from the overexcitabilities (OEs) in Dabrowski's Theory of Positive Disintegration. OEs are a set of *inborn* characteristics that come hand-in-hand for most people with advanced cognitive abilities. Many gifted children cope with these intensities and sensitivities in their family, school, and social situations.

The Polish psychologist and psychiatrist Kazimierz Dabrowski (1902-1980) created the concept of OEs.[9] Simply stated, OEs are a person's heightened ability to perceive and respond to stimuli— anything from an algebra problem to the seams in one's socks to a glorious sunset. There are five in total, and they break down as follows:

Emotional: Experiencing things deeply

Have you ever interpreted your child as overreacting to a perceived injustice that you know your neighbor's kid would take in stride? Does your child have surprisingly deep, personal relationships with people, animals, or even toys? Does your child alternate between joy and sadness with relative frequency?

Those are just some of the ways Emotional OE expresses itself.

These children are told that they are too sensitive and need to "toughen up." They are pathologized by well-meaning people who truly want to help but are not educated about gifted issues. While we do not want to overlook individuals who have real emotional issues and require diagnosis and treatment, we do not want to lump in children who are simply more intense into mistaken and detrimental diagnoses.

Emotional OE has its upside. Perhaps most powerful, Emotional OE is the source of your gifted child's amazing empathy. Have you ever been taken aback by your child's demonstration of care for another child who is hurting? In my opinion, this is the most wonderful way Emotional OE expresses itself.

Imaginational: Capacity to visualize, invent, and create

Imaginational OE is an inborn characteristic of many gifted children that expresses itself as unusually heightened imagination. Gifted children with this OE often have a hard time distinguishing between their fantasy and reality. They might have imaginary friends or create whole imaginary worlds. They sometimes have extra-vivid dreams that they can recall in detail. Imaginational OE is responsible for the creative and complex stories many gifted children dream up, and one of the reasons many will sit immersed in a pretend world of Lego for hours on end, for example. When harnessed, the Imaginational OE is a deep well of creativity.

Does your gifted child get wrapped up in his own inner world? Does he get himself into trouble for lying or exaggerating? When confronted, does he defend himself with such conviction that you find yourself believing him, despite having actual proof and knowing better? That is Imaginational OE getting your sweet baby into hot water. Can you imagine how this would not work in a traditional school setting?

Intellectual: Inquisitive and reflective

Does your child seem to have an insatiable curiosity, bombarding you with question after question? Does she philosophize on a range of topics from *Star Wars* to climate change to gender dynamics in the classroom? Do these musings sometimes take the form of rants and pontifications? Does she choose inopportune moments to make these thoughts known?

That is Intellectual OE driving many people crazy, sometimes earning your child a reputation as a pathological know-it-all and painting a target on her back for bullies.

Observing a child's passionate drive to learn can also be thrilling and contagious. My students with Intellectual OE inspire everyone around them to find joy in learning.

Psychomotor: Surplus of psychological and physical energy

Gifted children with Psychomotor OE have what seems like an inexhaustible supply of physical energy. While this could be said of most children, Psychomotor OE is different: It is an unusually enthusiastic zest for life. These children race through life in an attempt to experience the full amount of beauty and wonder the world has to offer. We place highly gifted children with non-verbal or visual-spatial learning styles, coping with Psychomotor OE in traditional, undifferentiated classrooms, and then we wonder why there are problems. In this scenario, troubling behaviors are bound to crop up.

Gifted children in these inappropriate scenarios are often described as "bouncing off the walls." They cannot stay still long enough to finish schoolwork. They have an extremely difficult time controlling the impulse to speak out of turn.

Notice that I wrote "inappropriate scenario." It is the situation or the learning environment that is flawed, not the learner. Sadly, a gifted child with Psychomotor OE is at risk for a misdiagnosis of ADD/ADHD in a school with professionals who are not acquainted with gifted traits.

Sensual: Heightened perception of everything related to the senses

Sensual OE is expressed as a heightened experience of sensual pleasure. Emotional artistic expression fills these children, whether in their sensitive and artistic reverence for the natural world, their deep wonder at a piece of art or music, or their desire to experience the world with all their senses.

And then there is the flip side. Often, because they also experience displeasure of the senses, these children may only wear certain obscure brands of socks or shirts without tags. I have noticed more than a few of them seem to go without underwear. Seriously.

As a teacher, I have to be careful what I eat for lunch (no sauerkraut—I love sauerkraut) and what hand lotion I use. Many of my students are "super-sniffers" and have a high sensitivity to aromas.

The presence of these intense passions and super-senses are hallmarks of sensual overexcitability. And it is the OE nearest and dearest to my heart.

OEs are something to accept, appreciate, and master, not to cure. They will never go away; they will rear their intense heads at the most inopportune times, even after lying dormant for long periods. Overexcitabilities enhance the texture of life. They bring an aliveness to the classroom. Without OEs the world would sadly be missing some of the most brilliant scientific breakthroughs, gorgeous paintings, and self-less humanitarians of history.

Gifted children may show deep compassion

Inequity is glaring in traditional schools. Socioeconomic status, gender, and race issues prevail and progress is slow going. I do not suggest that students be sheltered from these realities, but they must be empowered to influence positive change to these causes in a way that traditional school does not allow. Additionally, teasing is a huge affront to these sensitive students. Remarks that would roll off another student's back may stick in gifted students' sides like a thorn. This goes double if these students witness another student being teased. Many of these students have a meta-awareness of what is happening to the students around them, and this conjures a profoundly unsafe feeling.

Gifted children may be perfectionistic

There are worse things to be than perfectionistic. Linda Silverman once said to me, and I agree, "When harnessed, perfectionism can be quite useful when reaching for excellence."

In a classroom that teaches to those with average or less than average abilities, gifted children are not exposed to actual challenge and, therefore, not given the opportunity to harness their perfectionism. This can create unnecessary turmoil for gifted students later in life when faced with their first failures in college or otherwise.

Gifted children may display great curiosity

Gifted children have the ability to understand concepts with a depth beyond their years. This characteristic will prompt them to ask precocious, thought-provoking questions which teachers do not have the time (or perhaps the expertise) to explain.

Gifted children often prefer older companions/adults

Many of my students' creative play and games revolve around fantasy books above the reading level of age-mates. The rules to these games are extensive and complex. Older companions are more likely to meet my students where they are in their play and studies. This is why I match children in a program based on abilities and temperaments, not on age.

Gifted children may have a wide range of interests

Gifted children are passionate about learning on their own terms and about what is important to them. This passion and drive do not necessarily line up with today's education standards. Numerous gifted students have interests that lie outside what people generally think of as age-appropriate subject matter, such as war or uncommon diseases. The subjects they are passionate about learning may not easily relate to traditional academics. A gifted child may have a deep interest in coding or hacking, or may be driven to be an Olympic gymnast or an aerial silk artist in Cirque du Soleil. Gifted children will feel a drive to dive deep into these subjects until they know them at a sophisticated level, at which point, they may drop them like a hot potato and devour another subject

Gifted children may experience a deep mourning or loss when forced to stop learning about their preferred topic in order to sit down to do other work. One of my students in particular absolutely needed to finish his self-prescribed daily goal in math. He used an online program, which he loved. The more challenging the math became the more time he needed to meet his objective. If I pulled him away from math to transition into language arts, he simply could not be open to learning. It was obviously better for him to finish his math in his own time, after which he would happily work on other disciplines about which he felt less enthused.

Gifted children often display a great sense of humor

Advanced cognitive abilities include an advanced sense of humor that makes connections where other people do not or that call on the audience to have prior knowledge of esoteric subjects. It is easy to feel isolated when no one gets your jokes.

On the other hand, gifted children who are not having a fun and stimulating time in school may feel like they have no choice but to create their own fun and stimulation. When a child begins to find comfort in being the class clown, the adults will often begin to see that child as problem instead of searching for an underlying cause.

Gifted children can be highly creative

Another term for "highly creative" is "divergent thinking." Divergent thinkers think up numerous related ideas or solutions on any given topic or problem. Gifted children are known for this. They are the ones raising their hands asking if the Greek letter Omega looks like a penguin to anyone else, demanding to know during electronics class when the next zoology class is, and suggesting we build a robotic bird as our next class project. This process is creative, rebellious, chaotic, and, sadly, not respected in most traditional classrooms. Narrow, single discipline lessons that prefer an audial-sequential learning style do not generally make room for divergent thinking.

These students are famous for their abstract reasoning. My favorite story to tell about abstract thought processes come from when I was working through an activity with a profoundly gifted five-year-old. She was asked to label the house of ants "an anthill." With multiple pictures to choose from, including a teddy bear and a peanut butter and jelly sandwich, the student became quite confused. She thought the ants would most likely enjoy living in the peanut butter and jelly sandwich, as it would provide a source of food for them. It was difficult to argue with this logic, and honestly I did not try because it was easy to see her point of view.

What if this question had been part of a timed standardized test? I could see this child becoming immobilized by the vagueness of the answer choices, spiraling into anxiety about being wrong and ultimately choosing a supposedly incorrect answer. Standardized tests given by traditional schools do not measure this abstract thought process and, consequently, a large portion of today's college-bound students lack the ability to think abstractly. College professors have been vocal about high school graduates frustratingly incapable of making connections and inferences or thinking creatively and independently.[10,11]

A creative learning style calls for a creative learning environment. A traditional school setting which has been standardized to fit the average child's learning style is not going to work for gifted/2e children. They work best with complex subject matter delivered in a variety of ways and expressed through nontraditional methods. For instance, I once had a student write a three-act play about the scientific concepts of hydrophobic and hydrophilic molecules. Every one of my students was given the option to participate in the play, and they all did! More than likely this would not have happened in a traditional school.

When children are twice-exceptional—meaning they need advanced subject matter with support for their differences—problems within the learning environment become glaring. For example, dysgraphic children (children who have difficulty with writing) can still present their knowledge orally or through a video of their creation. This is not easily accommodated within a traditional classroom.

Gifted children often prefer to be independent learners

Group projects equal misery for gifted kids. Either they are seen as the most competent and get the lion's share of the work, or they work at a higher level and are angry that the other kids get to ride their coattails. Often, they are introverts who have a need to work independently. They enjoy the thrill of discovering things in their own way and time, and they resent having that taken away from them.

When you read over the above list of characteristics and examples, can you see how it would take a different kind of school to meet even the most basic needs for a gifted or twice-exceptional child? The benefits of creating an alternative learning environment for these children far outweigh the harm that can be caused by subjecting them to traditional school. By now, I hope you feel inspired to create a learning environment that screams, "You're appreciated! You're accepted! We want you here!" Gifted kids deserve it.

Chapter Three

Challenges, Philosophies, and Missions

In every micro-school I have ever participated, tension existed between balancing the various academic needs of my students within the context of their social-emotional learning and aligning that with the expectations of their parents.

That is quite a mouthful, I know. The complexity among these variables is made even more obvious when a child is gifted or twice-exceptional. Consider:

- The highly verbal child who reads and writes at a level worthy of a college class, but battles math anxiety so deep he can barely stand to add numbers in front of another human

- The child whose mechanical ingenuity knows no bounds beyond financial limitations, but she is eight years old and refuses to try reading and struggles to make friends

- The child who only wants to read, refusing all other schoolwork, not seeing the point of making friends because "books are his friends"

Depending on your outlook and the time of day, these children can be seen as a cause for celebration or deep worry. We love them and want to protect them. We want them to thrive in a world that can be harsh to outlier people.

The families in your community will be at different stages in accepting, understanding, and accommodating these differences. Even within a family, one parent may have one theory about how a child's temperament and education should be approached, while another may have a completely different theory. These differences can make for some tense dynamics in your micro-school.

Four main aspects need serious consideration and balancing when creating your own micro-school's mission and philosophy:

- **Students' temperaments.** How are you going to account for the different personalities, wants, and needs of your students? For example, some children will need a quiet space of calm, while others will want a rambunctious environment with plenty of visiting and movement.

- **Academic needs between students.** If one of your students demonstrates math abilities at a sixth grade level in the first grade, how are you going to meet her needs at the same time as other children who are not working at that level?

- **Parental expectations.** Sometimes, a caregiver's emotional baggage accrued from his time in school or other life events clouds his understanding of his or another child's capabilities. How will you approach this conflict when it arises?

- **Teaching preferences.** The way a teacher works best may not line up with what a student or parent needs. Will the teacher be flexible enough to incorporate feedback? Are the parents and students expectations of the teacher reasonable?

Balancing all of these needs will inevitably fall on the teacher and the other adults working in the micro-school. For the health and longevity of your program, teachers and administration must communicate clearly and consistently about the micro-school's expectations of the students and the caregivers.

In that vein, you have to decide on your pedagogical approach. What instructional approach do you prefer? Which approach will be best for the students in your program? Are you more inclined toward a classical education, or something project-based and hands-on? Perhaps you are attracted to something that looks more like a free school? Are you willing or able to change your approach if it would be a better match for your students?

Regardless of what you want, I implore you to take a long, hard look at what your students need and create the learning environment that will best meet those needs based on their requests. Be prepared to educate parents about the choices you make in the interest of their children's growth and development.

Put simply, teach students what they want and need to know in the way they want it and need it to be taught. You could end up with one student who prefers to study math on his own but checks in with you regularly for accountability, and another who needs a lot of engagement and examples to understand math. This can happen in the same space when people think creatively about what it means to learn as a group. Quieter students may listen to music with headphones to help them focus, while the teacher stays mindful to talk quietly with other students who need more engagement. Later, everyone might come together to play Minecraft during break.

Melanie Hayes, Ph.D., the founder and director of Big Minds Unschool for twice-exceptional children in Pinole, California has found a progressive model useful at her micro-school. As she said to me:

> In my experience, the children get this model right away. They feel it the minute they walk in the door: "Finally, a place I can learn and grow." Parents know it, too. They often cry with relief during their intake interview.

I will not sugar coat it for you—this is hard! Every adult participating in your micro-school will have to unpack his or her mental baggage about what "work" looks like and what it means to prove knowledge. There will be a push and pull between everyone's needs. For example, in the beginning of my career I was vocally against assessments. Through the push of parents, I began to realize that assessments do not need to be tests. They can be a chance for the teacher to understand if the child is on track with his learning agreement. They can be fun and interactive, as well as provide the students a chance to reflect on their learning in a positive way.

As I said in the introduction, "[Y]ou will sacrifice. Perhaps you will cry. And maybe you will just sit there numb, immobilized by stress." When that happens, think about the long-term ramifications if your students were to remain in their former situation. Was their love for learning being beaten out of them? Were they losing all self-confidence? Were they suppressing who they truly are or living in a constant state of overstimulation or anxiety? For many kids, your worst attempts to meet their needs will be better than the alternatives they have already encountered.

Talk with your students—a lot—about what they like and do not like about learning. Ask them what worked for them in their previous placements and what failed. Do they see a difference between education and learning? Make this a collaborative process.

The objectives of the mission for your micro-school could be seen as a continuum, with one side focused on academics and achievements and the other on social emotional learning. I prefer a balanced approach where academics and social emotional learning weigh equally. There is a time and place to focus on each, and this can often be done at the same time.

Based on my deeply held values for creativity, freedom, and choice, I advocate openly for a progressive approach to learning in micro-schools. This means using inquiry and problem-solving as means to help children learn to drive their intrinsic motivation. To learn more about what progressive education is and is not, have a look at Alfie Kohn's books and blog at www.alfiekohn.org.

One example of how I put my values into action is during the Independent Project Time (IPT). For IPT, children are asked to pick any subject or topic they like, learn as much as they can about that subject, and create a product that communicates what is most important to them about that subject. These products can be anything from a performance to a Lego creation to a five-paragraph essay. The point is for the learning and the product to be meaningful to the student, not something assigned or tested by the teacher.

In the summer of 2014, I attended SENG's (Supporting the Emotional Needs of the Gifted) annual conference. While there, I took a workshop with some friends and colleagues on the powerful use of improvisational comedy for team building in schools. I can be a rather shy student and had come to class mainly to observe. The joy and intelligence of the woman running the workshop was infectious and, before I knew it, I was playing pretend like a second grader alongside everyone else. It was great! I realized that facilitating independent projects is a lot like participating in an improvisational comedy class. It is one big game of "yes, and _____." For those of you unfamiliar with this improvisational theatre game, one participant accepts what the other has created, usually around a theme like "cars" or "going to the beach" and adds something to it. The game might run something like:

Student: *I want to build a catapult.*

Teacher: *Yes, and what do you already know about catapults?*

Student: *I will need to do some research, because I only know that I think they're cool.*

Teacher: *Yes, and I am here to help you find some accurate and reputable source materials. I always wondered, what's the difference between a catapult and a trebuchet?*

Another aspect of my facilitation of micro-schools is founded in the tradition of Nonviolent Communication or NVC (see *Resources*). One of the fundamentals of this communication practice is to approach behaviors and choices with curiosity. If a child or a caregiver is making a choice that I do not understand, I do my best to suspend judgment, not jump to a conclusion. Instead, I openly ask "Why?" For this to be effective, my question must come from a place of true curiosity rather than an adversarial stance. This is no easy task, and when I forget, I find that an open discussion and apology go far to repair the damage done.

The best way to inspire social-emotional intelligence is to model it. Respect a child's need for autonomy and choice, and you will be pleasantly surprised by the ripple effect this has throughout your community. Take the time to have a restorative process when conflict arises. Approach intensity with curiosity. This is the path to meet educational needs regardless of the subject matter. The example below illustrates a typical conversation I might have with a twice-exceptional student with dysgraphia, a learning disability that affects a person's capability to write coherently with a pencil or pen:

(A teacher passes out blank sheets of scratch paper for note-taking or drawing. She makes no requests about writing.)

Student: *(Immediately agitated)* WE HAVE TO WRITE? YOU'RE GOING TO MAKE US WRITE?

Teacher: *(Calmly, after a couple of seconds) I'm surprised to hear you say that. Have I ever made you write before?*

Student: *(Slightly more calm) Well, I'm not writing! You can't make me!*

Teacher: *It's important to you to know that you don't have to write if you don't want to. Am I hearing that correctly?*

Student: *Yeah!*

Teacher: *OK, you don't have to write if you don't want to. I have seen you draw about the things we discuss in class. You're more than welcome to continue doing that. Another option is to type in a Google doc and share it with me. Or you could play with your therapy putty. [Often used with students who have dysgraphia so they can build hand strength.]*

Later I might have a general discussion about the importance of writing as a skill. My choice will depend on what I am observing in my students that day, and if they seem up for a talk.

Some children will catch on quicker than others. Everyone should remain mindful of the mission, stay firm and kind in their values, and approach each other with curiosity when intensity inevitably knocks on the door.

Chapter Four
Recruiting Families

Although this chapter focuses on how to spread the news of your program and recruit families, it tangentially addresses advocating for gifted and twice-exceptional children. Building a sustainable micro-school means getting out there and telling the world about what your community is going through—not easy in a world where myths about gifted people and gifted education are accepted as truths. A big part of this work is combating these inaccurate and damaging myths, such as "Gifted children will be fine on their own" or "Aren't all gifted children supposed to get straight As?" Your students may have received unqualified and unrequested diagnoses from family members like "I think your kid has ADHD" or "This kid can't be gifted; she clearly has a learning disability."

If the population of people who understand what it means to be gifted is small, the subgroup of people who understand twice-exceptionality is even smaller. Twice-exceptionality exists. And keep in mind, gifted children experience a high misdiagnosis rate for ADHD or Oppositional Defiant Disorder (ODD), when what they are really coping with are overexcitabilities.[12] The line between twice-exceptionality and overexcitabilities can be blurry.

Do not be tempted to hide your micro-school venture to avoid disapproving looks and ignorant comments. Get out there, loud and proud. Your future students need this. By taking a stand and creating the learning environment you know these children need, you could inspire many others to learn about gifted and twice-exceptional children. Gifted and twice-exceptional families tend to isolate themselves. How many times have you wished you could find a peer for your child or an understanding friend for yourself?

I have devised a beginner's marketing and networking outline so you can begin promoting your micro-school. Feel free to use it as is or modify it to fit your needs and goals.

Step One

Determine what the homeschool and private school laws are in your state. For true clarity and peace of mind seek out an attorney. It is good to have a relationship with one if you plan to move forward with your own program. This book is not meant to be legal advice and is provided for informational purposes only. In the meantime, you can check your state's homeschool laws at Ann Zeise's website, A2Zhomeschooling.com.

Website

You want your website to be as professional and clear as possible. At the very least it must include:

- Your school's name
- Your school's mission
- Class offerings and schedule
- Teacher information and biographies
- Contact information
- Blog

Consider the blog portion of your website as your chance to share your point of view and connect with like-minded families and professionals. It also provides a self-screening filter: When families read your thoughts about educating and parenting gifted or twice-exceptional students, they will either clap with joy or move on. To save time and energy, you only want those who clap with joy to contact you about you program. In the resource section, I have listed some of my favorite blogs written by parents and educators of gifted children to get you started and inspired.

Your Local Community

Anyone who wants to build a sustainable micro-school will need to familiarize themselves with the local gifted community of professionals who understand giftedness and twice-exceptionality. These professionals can refer families to your program. Take some time to network and market yourself and your micro-school to promote enrollment and educate the public about what you are doing. The professionals page on the GHF website is a great starting point for finding people in your area of interest.

If you already have a relationship with doctors or therapists who understand what it means to be gifted or twice-exceptional, make sure they are aware of your new project. If these professionals believe in what you are offering, they may help by promoting your project through their own social media outlets. Provide them with a simple flyer that they can hang in their offices advertising your program.

An effective flyer should have a short summary of the program and the community it hopes to serve. Make the design consistent with your website. This helps to create continuity and recognition among the people following your work. The flyer should also include contact information and perhaps a testimonial from one or two of the families with whom you are currently working.

To find families in your local community, reach out to local gifted meet-up groups. If you are not already a member of one, you can search for them online, including Yahoo Groups, Google Groups, and Facebook. Try organizing a meet-up or park day for families to learn more about your idea.

Online

Having and maintaining your website/blog is only the beginning of your online life. Now get online and promote yourself!

Use Facebook, Twitter, and Pinterest (and whatever other social media sites you discover reach your potential market). Regularly and frequently connect with people all over the world about the issues related to giftedness and twice-exceptionality. Keep in mind that *people will move for an established program that is doing good things.* That is how rare excellent programs for these families are.

Introduce and align yourself with the major online gifted and twice-exceptional organizations, particularly GHF and SENG. Also, look for others doing the same work. Every so often I check out #alted on Twitter to find people interested in alternative education. Many of the followers of #alted are excited to chat and are supportive of others who want to increase awareness of alternative education.

Above all, the program's reputation and the positive recommendations of others are major contributors to your program's longevity. Word-of-mouth has always been the number one way that families have found me. Most of the time, they have heard from a friend that I am running a good program, next they see a small flier or my card at a local gathering place for families, then they go to my website and read my blog to see if their vision aligns with mine. Interested families seem to know all about me before we even meet!

Screening Process

You will need a system for screening families to be sure they are a good fit for your program. Not every gifted and twice-exceptional family's goals and needs will align with your mission and philosophy. Not to worry. Maybe they will buy a copy of this book and create a program that aligns with *their* vision. Stay true to your ideals to avoid drama down the road.

During your screening process, keep in mind that small differences are inevitable. Watch out for big differences, such as views about respect and compliance. You also want to be sure the student's ability and social style will gel (or has the potential to gel) with your current students'.

Families typically email me as a first line of contact. Next, either I or a parent from our community schedules a phone conversation with the main caregiver in the family. We chat about the child's interests, what wasn't working in their old placement, how they heard about the program, and what they are hoping to get out of a program like mine. I view these phone interviews as a chance to get the big, scary questions out of the way. As part of the conversation, you should consider asking tough questions such as:

- Has your child ever displayed aggressive behaviors (e.g., hitting, biting, throwing things, threats, and cursing) toward a teacher or administrator?

- Has your child displayed this behavior toward other children?

- Do you fear your child may be suicidal or engaging in self-harm, including cutting, eating disorders, etc.?

These are hard questions to ask, and even harder questions to answer. But, if you fail to ask them, you may get into a situation that will make you wish you had asked. Make sure the caregivers you speak with know that you are not judging them. A "yes" answer to any of these questions does not have to mean the child is automatically ineligible for the program. You need to know these things if you are going to support your students effectively.

Prospective families may want to know more about your current student population. Be careful to maintain the privacy of your current students and their families when talking to prospective families. I explain my students in hypothetical terms and broad strokes to interested families.

Home Visits

Depending on how I assess the family during the phone interview, I will schedule a home visit. For instance, if they answer yes to any of the tough questions above, but those incidents happened in the past, I will take the time to meet the child face-to-face before the family visits the program. I will also schedule a home meeting if a child is deeply introverted or shy. That child will have an easier time visiting the program when he has a friendly face he recognizes.

When I go into a family's home, I usually spend most of my time with the child. I ask to see children's rooms. Kids love showing off their rooms! I show interest in their interests. Above all, I approach them with warm curiosity. This is my time to get a sense if a child is going to be open to me as their teacher and if he is going to get along with my other students.

Shadow Days

If everything goes well, I schedule two shadow days. I usually need two full days of having potential students in my classroom to determine if they are going to be happy there. When the shadow days are scheduled, prepare your current students for a visitor by explaining to them the behaviors you hope to see. Prep them on how to talk to new people. Remind them how it feels to be a newcomer.

Because I do not know the child well enough to create an individual learning plan, I ask that the parents provide some activities for their child to do while the students are completing their learning agreements. Bringing a book is an excellent idea. Have all your students bring a book, for that matter. Sometimes, a student will want their parent to hang around until she feels comfortable. Sometimes, a parent will hang close by in a coffee shop and be "on call." These are all agreements that you will need to work out with the parent beforehand.

For my last program, a parent created the following needs and wants list for assessing family compatibility. I typically give this to parents before the shadow day. Evaluate their answers against the answers of your current families. Are there any big conflicts? Do your families have a three where the new family has a one, or vice versa? Is it an area that will be a deal breaker for you or them? Be explicit when these areas of differences are revealed. Everyone needs to know when they are making compromises so that expectations are clear.

Child's name:
Caregiver's name:
Please rank each objective's importance:
3 - Very Important, 2 - Moderately Important, 1 - Not Important

	Fostering a sense of ownership in the learning process
	Open-ended time for creative exploration/physical play
	Structured time for specific academic areas
	Developing a positive sense of self
	Feeling like a valued member of a community
	Providing structure to support homeschooling goals
	Learning collaboratively
	Learning in the company of others, but not necessarily with others
	Developing critical thinking skills/habits of mind (process focus)
	Developing general knowledge in subject areas (content focus)
	Completing in-depth units of study
	Finding enjoyment in learning
	Calm, disruption-free learning space
	Meeting grade level standards
	Assessments to monitor growth
	Social-emotional learning

Please number content areas in order of importance:
__ Math Support   __ Arts & Crafts
__ Science Instruction   __ Design Thinking
__ History Instruction   __ Writing
__ Literature/Reading Comprehension __ Computer Science/Programming

After two days of successful shadowing, I have another meeting with the family. If we all want to move forward, I give them a contract, collect a deposit and first month's tuition, and we're off!

One thing you may notice: I do not require families to provide IQ or any assessments to prove their child's giftedness or twice-exceptionality. If they happen to have them, I like to look at them. The information can be helpful, but I do not require them. Many families simply cannot afford testing like that, or they have received testing from unskilled assessors and the results to do not accurately relate the child's abilities. I trust my sense of a child above all else. If I think my program can serve a child and the family is a fit, we go for it.

When you begin with a new family, it can feel like an emergency. Parents need to work; maybe the kids are bored and restless at home. You may be tempted to bring in any new family to bolster the finances of your program. Resist the pressure. Take your time to do it right and everyone will benefit.

Chapter Five
Choosing a Lead Educator

Your lead educator will be the lynchpin of your entire micro-school. Finding one who can gracefully balance the needs and expectations of a micro-school's community can be difficult and time-consuming. I have ended up with the bulk of the responsibility in my past programs because it was terribly difficult to find educators who met my and the program's families' standards. Your limited budget often will pay for only one teacher, at least initially. Perhaps you may have someone in your group who is excited to take on the role of lead educator. Great! Regardless of where you find your educator, if you plan to recruit families from outside your current community, your teacher will need to have the ability to speak confidently about her or his practices and philosophies.

Is it important that your teacher candidate understands her or his own giftedness or twice-exceptionality? The fact that I am twice-exceptional has always been an important aspect in terms of building a connection with interested families. Parents and caregivers like that I have first-hand experience overcoming the same obstacles their children are facing. It will be up to you to determine if this will be a significant qualifier for your candidate.

Should your candidates feel comfortable opening up about their struggles and triumphs as a gifted/2e person? Have they integrated useful practices and habits of mind to harness their overexcitabilities? Are they self-aware and self-responsible? I am a fairly blunt person and will ask directly in an interview, "Can you tell me about your self-awareness and the strategies you use to cope with stress?" These children are intense; they will push an otherwise reasonable adult to the edge. When under fire, a person lacking in self-connection will find herself behaving in less than dignified ways. These qualities will determine who will be successful as an educator in your micro-school better than a teaching degree alone.

Do not limit your search to people with teaching degrees and experience in traditional classrooms. What you are creating is non-traditional, and the kind of indoctrination that comes along with a teaching degree steeped in a traditional mindset can take some time to undo. Not to say it cannot be undone, but that undoing creates tension. In particular, potential micro-school teachers need to undo their ideas about assessments, grade levels, respect, and appropriate classroom behavior. Building a micro-school is an intense enough experience on its own, without adding the need to retrain a teacher.

On the other hand, many teachers who work in or have retired from traditional classrooms are done with the traditional way. They itch for the opportunity to be more effective. Stay open. The successful candidate will likely look nothing like what you have pictured in your mind. You may have to compromise some aspect of your vision of the "right" teacher. Prepare yourself for that by making a list of optional and non-optional attributes of your ideal teacher. For example, should she be bilingual? Have a background in the humanities or the sciences? Experience with gifted/2e children? What are you willing to train?

Also consider each candidate's:

- familiarity with the age group of your micro-school

- experience with special needs

- administrative experience

- style of communication

- view of parents' role

- experience creating curriculum

Once you have created a profile of your ideal educator, let the world know, online and through word of mouth, that you are looking for interested educators. Designate a point person to receive inquiries and organize interviews.

Teaching Philosophy

Whomever you consider for the role of lead educator should be able to produce a clearly and decisively written teaching philosophy. If she has one available as part of her resume package, all the better. If she does not, have the teacher write one before she is interviewed. If the teacher is willing, you may want to workshop this important piece of writing together. This document will help your teacher communicate effectively about what she has to offer students in the classroom. Keep in mind that this is a living document that the teacher is meant to update as experience is accrued. A teaching philosophy should answer questions such as:

- What is the teacher's concept of learning?

- What are the teacher's goals in the classroom?

- How does the teacher plan to interact with students?

- What methods does the teacher employ?

- How does the teacher plan to develop professionally?

- How does the teacher view assessments, standardized testing, grade level standards, and the role of homework?

If your candidate does not have a written teaching philosophy, you can use the questions outlined above as interview questions. Assess your candidates for openness, enthusiasm, and excitement. The learning curve is steep. Remember that what you are doing is very "out of the box" and whoever ends up as your lead educator will need time and compassion as she finds her footing in this new role.

As I am not one to make others do what I am unwilling to do, I have included my teaching philosophy. If you agree with any of my positions on education, feel free to use them to guide your process as your write your own teaching philosophy or as you support someone else as they write theirs.

When I talk about learning, I am talking about learning how to learn. I want my students to become well-acquainted with their intrinsic motivation and how to use their strengths to overcome their limitations. The learning environment that I create will show children how to look at themselves and the world with a healthy critical eye in their path to self-actualization.

Through attachment-based teaching, I create a tribe of learning in my program. We value choice, partnership, and autonomy by encouraging self-directed learning through inquiry-based projects. I employ project-based learning with an emphasis on design thinking. My students ask themselves questions like "What question am I trying to answer?" and "What problem am I trying to solve?" I draw heavily from the magnanimous qualities of improvisational theatre. Also important is the integration of technology as a tool to extend learning and prepare students to be effective digital citizens.

Mastery is not a cold list of objectives that can be demonstrated at the teacher's whim. Mastery is the sense of satisfaction that children feel when they have acquired the skills and knowledge they hoped for. I want to encourage a love of learning, as well as a love of self and the world around them. I believe that children who feel secure in who they are can take thoughtful risks that lead to useful innovations.

My role is that of a facilitator who makes space for deep learning that leads to mastery. At my very best, I work in partnership with students and maintain standards of safety and intellectual excellence while they learn what they wish. When challenges arise, I adopt a more authoritative approach. I maintain firm and kind boundaries with empathy, while providing explanations for the limits I think are necessary.

In the classroom, an ideal teacher-student interaction will begin with the student. The student will know what she wants to learn, will have the skills to make a plan, and will have the confidence to ask for and accept feedback. While the plan is executed, the student will have the social-emotional skills to seek support and advice when things go wrong or require redirection. The student will feel excited to share with the group what she has learned, and will either extend or begin a new project. It is my goal that my students develop skills that will free them to speak, write, or otherwise demonstrate knowledge about whatever they wish.

Topics for study as a group are selected democratically through instant run-off voting. Together, we develop a plan of study. The scaffolding of Bloom's taxonomy is manipulated at will to meet the individual needs of students. Student-designed rubrics are used by the students so they can hold themselves accountable as their projects progress and know when they have met their goals.

How learning is demonstrated and assessments are administered is agreed upon between my students and me ahead of time. I administer formative assessments to track student's progress. These could be as informal as my recording my observations of students while they work or pulling daily work for a portfolio, or as formal as requesting those students complete a written progress report and create a formal presentation. Along the way, goals of learning may change or diverge, which is healthy and normal. Flexibility for that is inherent in my learning environment's model.

I see grades as an unnecessary, ineffective, and antiquated method of determining progress. This is a point of view I have held since the second grade, when I received my first C in math, despite my efforts. Grades do not reflect how hard a student has worked and are therefore not interesting to me. That being said, if grading is useful to an individual student's process, I will happily oblige. This is the level of flexibility in the classroom to which I am committed.

I have a powerful drive to learn new things and partner with students who want the same. My regard for empathy and exploration in the classroom is founded in my deepest commitment to my values of freedom and creativity. I see a direct, natural, and easeful correlation between the growth of children into thoughtful, self-directed people and the growth of positive social change.

I intend to grow as a teacher first and foremost through the feedback of my students. Their comfort level, their willingness to take risks to learn, is how I know I am on track. It is important to me to stay current on the social and scientific theories of neuro-diversity. I seek out the support and collaboration of other alternative educators online and in-person. Most important, I stay clear and attuned to my sense of intuition about any given student. My intuition is my most powerful asset an educator.

Treating Educators Fairly

Keep in mind that the educators of your micro-school have an increased chance of being exploited, intentionally or unintentionally. Independent contractors have few labor laws and no unions to protect them. A socially responsible micro-school will:

- Pay its employees as well as it possibly can. Do not nickel and dime this aspect of your program. Teaching gifted and 2e children can be some of the most difficult teaching in the world. If you pay a minimum wage, you will end up with a minimum job. And you know you want something better than that for your students.

- Be sure employees are adequately supported with an assistant, so they can take breaks as needed. Consider using a co-op model to have parents rotate as assistants. This carries its own risk because parents have a learning curve accepting other children's special needs as those impact their own child. You can prepare assistants and volunteers by requesting they read or take part in a training session on your program's mission.

- Respect teachers' off hours. Only contact them by telephone if it is an emergency or if they express a preference for it. Otherwise, use email.

- Pay employees for planning time, whether during school hours or after.

- Have a substitute contingency plan, paid sick days, etc.

Creating and sustaining a micro-school, particularly in the first years, is like living in a pressure cooker, making it easy to cross boundaries unintentionally and enter unhealthy relationships. Establish respectful boundaries by detailing your expectations in writing. Show your educator appreciation both tangibly and intangibly. Your efforts will help create a healthy, sustainable micro-school.

Chapter Six
Logistics, Environment, and Schedules

Many children feel overwhelmed when they enter the typical classroom. Alongside 20 to 30 children and their desks is the clutter of supplies, books, student work, and informational posters from floor to ceiling. Add to that the buzzing of fluorescent lighting hovering around their ears like an invisible gnat, the smells that naturally occur when that many people occupy a space for more than a couple of hours, and the classroom can feel like an assault to a sensitive child before he has even found his seat!

Sensitive gifted and twice-exceptional children benefit from a calm, neutral environment. Consider the following parameters before committing to the space that will house your micro-school. Remember, the omission of one or two of these should not deter you from moving forward with your own micro-school. Not all gifted children require all of these in a learning environment. Work with your people to prioritize what is most important.

Class Size

Class sizes must be kept small, with student-to-teacher ratios of four to six students to one teacher. That teacher should have an assistant for when conflict or intensity arises among students.

The class cannot be composed of just any four to six gifted kids who come your way. They do not have to match in age, but they must be close in ability, academically and socially-emotionally. More than anything, they need to be around actual peers, not just age-mates.

Classroom Needs

Desks in rows will not do. Comfy learning areas with couches and lap desks with opportunities to work at big tables together with computers are best. Waist-high tables at which students can stand are also great. I love the Montessori approach of having small rugs where children can lay out on the floor to delineate working areas.

You will need a lot of outlets. If you lack a technology budget, have students bring laptops from home. Earbuds or headphones are a must to keep down the noise level that occurs when students are working on independent projects. Boundaries about how laptops are used during break times and what will happen if a child is seen using the computer in a way other than what was agreed upon will need to be discussed from day one. Work with your community to determine what the consequences are if misuse of technology occurs.

Fill your space with as many books, lab and art supplies, and technologies as possible. These supplies must be carefully organized and easily accessible. Rotate items in and out of the space. If students are not using certain books or supplies, move those into storage and bring them back out as the needs of your group change. Do this when nobody is around to avoid disputes about what should stay and what should go. If someone notices that something is missing and requests bringing it back for a project or something else, I happily acquiesce.

Your location should be somewhere safe with relatively low traffic. Ideally, the kids will have an outdoor play area with some kind of play structure or large field for sports or other games. You could consider a public park within walking distance where you can play. Avoid being by businesses that create disruptive sounds and smells. (My last space was located near a restaurant, which was very bad for some students' olfactory sensitivities.) Consider the nearby businesses' needs. Will they be disrupted by the normal noisiness that occurs when children are excited about learning? Some gifted and twice-exceptional children are prone to explosive behavior. Try to locate your space in a more remote place to avoid disturbing other businesses.

These suggestions take for granted that you have the budget to pay for the overhead of a rented space and can cover all of the costs associated with preparing and maintaining that space. My last space was donated to me by the parents of one of my students, and it was wonderful! Look around your community. Who has a basement or other seldom-used portion of their home that could be converted? Do any of them have a business that is closed some portion of the week? What about your church? Keep in mind that using a space like these may affect the terms of the insurance policies for these spaces. Be sure to investigate that before committing to anything. Get creative with what is available and you will be surprised how happy you can be with what you have! Keep in mind that the smaller the space, the fewer families you can serve.

Classroom Maintenance

Now for the hardest part: Inspiring your students to keep the space clean and organized. The amount of mess in a micro-school seems to be directly proportional to the amount of learning that is happening. One mistake I always make is not scheduling clean up time in between lessons or scheduled transitions. Don't do as I do! A mess may be a sign of learning, but that same mess can also contribute to over-stimulation. It is a difficult balancing act that you will have to work out over time. I suggest carefully planning the layout of your learning space and making sure that everything has an accessible and maintainable place. Take pictures of each area of the classroom in its most pristine state and place the pictures next to those areas. Now the children have a visual reference when it is time to clean up.

What about projects in progress? Make space for a project area with individually labeled shelves for students to store those partially completed projects. Accept that this area will become the graveyard for half-finished projects. Do your best to have children take home, recycle, or throw away (good luck) projects that have sat around for longer than a couple of weeks.

Find a way to divide your space into quiet and active zones. If possible, create an additional extra, small, private area made comfortable for resting for when a student reaches her limit and needs some space or a conference with a caring adult. Keep in mind that different tasks require different levels of concentration and different children have different sensory needs when it comes to noise and activity levels.

As an aside, I always allow students to learn shoe-free. I also keep multiple flavors of gum on hand. These little touches go far in helping your students settle into a space and feel welcome.

Designing Your Classroom

Lighting is an important and often overlooked aspect of children's learning. Because a large portion of our sensory input happens through our eyes, it is important to make sure children see with comfort. When children have an extra level of sensitivity associated with learning differences and sensory challenges, like most twice-exceptional children, attention to lighting becomes critical. Since the current running through a fluorescent bulb is not constant, lights flicker and hum at a level almost imperceptible to most people, especially adults. Fluorescents also produce a cool light from a narrow spectrum. Switching from fluorescent lighting to full-spectrum lighting is proven to help reduce agitation, increase focus, and alleviate symptoms brought on by Seasonal Affective Disorder (SAD).[13] I have heard reports of many gifted classrooms calming down quite a bit once the teacher relied on natural light from windows or switched the bulbs from fluorescent to full-spectrum lighting.

Color is another aspect of the classroom that calls for careful consideration. Bright, warm colors are stimulating, but what if you have a child who is easily over-stimulated? In that case, you will want to avoid the traditional primary color scheme in favor of something cool, neutral, and calming. Light blues, natural wood, and a lot of natural light are ideal in a micro-school for gifted children. To get a better idea of what this can look like, schedule a tour of a traditional Montessori classroom.

Displaying work the students feel proud of can be nice, but it can get out of hand. I suggest creating an agreement early on with the students. Explain that because space is limited, displayed work must be cycled out of the classroom as new work is created and displayed. I also keep a standing file box with file folders dedicated to each child and the various subjects being studied for finished and in-progress school work. Curious parents and professionals who work with your students appreciate seeing their children's work.

The learning environment should also be as scent-free as possible. Scents can trigger migraines and interfere with concentration.

Designing Your Daily Schedule

Before deciding what you are going to study and what your daily schedule is going to be, you should first understand your students. If they are just coming out of a traditional schooling situation that has not worked for them, do not expect them to happily jump into a alternative learning environment and know what to do. They need to decompress. To help smooth this transition, many children need to deschool, meaning they need downtime to undo the unhealthy psychological mindsets that many gifted and twice-exceptional children develop in traditional school. A commonly held belief in alternative education is that a child needs one month of deschooling for each year spent in traditional school. This is not a hard-and-fast rule; how long your individual students need depends on them and what they have been through. Deschoolers need a lot of down time, with time spent pursuing their own interests in their own way. This is the time for these children to reconnect with who they really are outside of the classroom. An even more flexible micro-school schedule may be needed at first, with more fixed expectations put in place down the line.

For your daily schedule, I suggest you have a soft start and a flexible plan.

Arrival

Children should arrive by 8:45 for a 9:00 a.m. start time. Morning routines can be difficult for some children and having a flexible arrival time gives families more transition time resulting a smoother day. I have had school days that started as late as 10:00 a.m. Arrival and start times should work for the families involved in the micro-school. Some families will have childcare needs that extend beyond the normal school day hours; hiring an additional person for childcare can be negotiated within the group.

Check-in

Every day should start with a group check-in meeting. Ideally, students take turns sharing with the group how they are, what they are excited about, and what has disappointed them. This is also a good time to go over the daily schedule and remind students of the group learning expectations.

Beyond this you can schedule your day however your community sees fit. You should discuss this at length before the first day of school. Once you get started, if the chosen plan is not working, have another meeting incorporating the requests of the students and change it. This is the beauty of a micro-school: if any aspect of it is not working, you have the autonomy to shift things until it does.

Work Periods

I usually schedule three work periods, 45 minutes to one-and-a-half hours in length, for children to work on learning objectives either within the group or individually with guidance. In the past, I have scheduled fifteen-minute breaks, but the transition in and out of a small break like that is usually more trouble than it is worth. Instead, I suggest allowing children to take small breaks, individually, when they need them.

Based on your discussions with families and others in your micro-school community, you may want every work period to be focused on group learning around a particular subject. Or you may want to have every work period dedicated to children's individual projects. You could also have a hybrid of the two with the morning work period dedicated to individual math and language arts work, the next work period focused on a subject that has been agreed upon by the students in a democratic fashion, and the third devoted to individual projects. Of course, in the middle of the day you should schedule a generous lunch and play time.

Field Trips

One day of the month could be set aside for a group outing to a museum or another fun and enriching place. The sensitivity of your students will be something to consider when you plan your outings. A break in routine with its unknowns could create all kinds of stress and anxiety for some of the students involved. If the children are up for outings, schedule them ahead of time so you can secure chaperones, drivers, and other volunteers, as well as reserve tours and the like.

Presentations

Along with monthly outings I suggest having a reoccurring presentation day. One morning a month or every other month ask the children to give a five- to 10-minute presentation on their individual projects or something they are working on outside of school. Parents and extended family should be invited to attend. Turn these days into little celebrations by bringing in treats and giving each student a small gift, like fun erasers or stickers with a card that lets them know how proud of them you are. I do not grade my students, so presentation day gives my students something tangible to work towards and a chance to show to their families what they have accomplished. Presentation day meets the need for accountability with much more integrity than a grade. Prepare children in advance for these presentations by scheduling practice sessions and time for supporting the organization of your students' individual presentations.

I have seen amazing leaps of confidence in my students as a result of these presentations. Initially, knowing how sensitive my students are, I was nervous to incorporate presentations into our routine. Then I saw the healing that could occur when a student felt seen and heard by his community about his passions, and now I am sold. Try it out. You can always change your mind if it is not working for your program.

Breaks

Some children are not going to be able to follow this plan, and all children will have at least a few days when they cannot follow this plan. When a student needs space to do her own thing, I am inclined to give it to her. Dancing around these expectations and boundaries is an art, honed with time. Make sure everyone is on the team by including everyone in the discussion when plans need to shift. Communicate with parents as needed through text and email. They appreciate the updates and access to their children's daily happenings in real time.

Do not forget to plan for teacher and assistant breaks. These can be scheduled during lunch and other breaks or during work periods taught by specialty teachers.

Depending on the needs of your group and the requirements of the space, you could micro-school year-round. I take summers off now, but in the beginning of my career, I would run summer camps that were a lot like our yearly programs, but with even more freedom.

Contracts

I am not an attorney, and I strongly suggest you seek the counsel of an attorney before setting out on this adventure. An attorney can help you create a binding contract, as well as advise you on the other facets of running a micro-school.

Because this will be a small group of families who will no doubt bond and find familiarity within the group, you may be tempted to skip over contracts and agreement-making, thinking to yourself, "Surely they'll keep their word." *Do not make this mistake.*

A contract does more than protect, it makes it real. There is a symbolism and a ritual to a contract that makes people reflect and ask if they are making the right decision. This is the level of reflection that you want in your community. It also shows the families you are working with that you are serious about this endeavor and are taking steps to ensure its sustainability.

Take the time to sit down with families and explain every facet of the contract to them. When a family enters my program, I require a deposit of one month's tuition. Families are also required to provide thirty days' notice when intending to quit the program. When the thirty days begin, they may apply this deposit to their last month's tuition. The deposit and policy serve two purposes, it inspires families to carefully consider their reasoning for wanting to leave a program and it protects the financial stability of the overall program.

In the appendices, I've included two copies of individual contracts, one that I used and one that my friend and colleague Dr. Melanie Hayes uses. These are for reference only. Although I expect you to borrow heavily from them, retain your own attorney for approval of such important documents.

Chapter Seven
Parents and Fostering Community

You will find that though your work centers on gifted children, you actually spend a lot of time working with gifted families. Parents would learn about my micro-school and come to me stressed out and with a million questions. At some point in our conversations, they would realize they were not only asking about how to best support their children, they were also asking about how to best support themselves and their partners.

A clinical understanding of giftedness as a holistic, inherent cognitive difference has only now begun to enter popular culture. There are pockets of people working hard to develop strategies to support the gifted learner. The semi-joking question I get from gifted parents all the time is, "Where were you when I was five?"

Micro-schools can offer an entire family respite and a chance to share triumphs and struggles with a community of supportive peers, if they let it. Take note of the qualification of "if they let it." Gifted parents are often just as intense and sensitive as their children, possibly never experiencing the celebration and acceptance their child enjoys in a micro-school. Growing up in a world that classified them as "too much" and "too intense" means they likely developed some unhealthy coping mechanisms just to make it through this world, mechanisms like micro-managing and tendency to act arrogantly. Though I have compassion for that, I have also seen how a parent's lack of understanding and acceptance of his or her gifted/2e identity or that of his or her child's can sour an entire program.

I have also worked with families who have children that seem like they came out of nowhere. Parents who were rule-followers and made straight As have a child who bounces around, seems to live to break rules, and does not care about grades or achievement.

Often families have a child who reminds them of their younger brother or sister who was always in trouble. These parents are deeply concerned for their child because they remember how their sibling was ostracized and subsequently internalized this shame and made unhealthy life choices. This is the sad path of many divergent gifted and twice-exceptional people, and these parents are terrified that this may also be the path for their child.

Some of your parents will be evolved, responsible people. They will have a handle on who they are and who their child is. They will show appreciation and support whenever they can. Naturally, they can have their challenging moments like we all do, but they know how to apologize and learn from their transgressions.

Overall, everyone will be in a different place when it comes to accepting their children's quirks. This difference will cause caregivers to struggle with compassion for the entire community. Some parents want their quirky kids to be with peers who maybe are not so quirky, hoping that some of that mythical normalness will rub off on their children. This rarely works out the way parents want it to, and usually backfires in a painful way for their children. Children sense the subliminal lack of acceptance from their parents and will not connect with the less quirky children because of differences in paradigms and abilities.

Coming Together and Playing Nice

To help all these different families with different needs in different stages of their lives come together as a functioning, supportive community, you need to set a plan in place. Start by creating a clear outline about how and to whom parents will address concerns. Make this plan available in writing.

Agree not to gossip about each other or each other's children. Parents may be tempted to find fault in other student's quirkiness out of fear that such quirkiness reflects negatively on their own child. Claim a high level of integrity in all of your program's communication. I like the T.H.I.N.K. method and suggest all adults ask the following questions about their communications before offering it to others:

- Is it **T**rue?

- Is it **H**elpful?

- Is it **I**nspiring?

- Is it **N**ecessary?

- Is it **K**ind?

If what you are about to say does not meet at least three of these requirements, keep it for your journal.

If you can, schedule regular times to come together outside of the micro-school to do something fun and to get to know each other beyond your role as caregivers. You should also schedule regular group meetings to discuss the growth of and any changes to your program.

Consider scheduling workshops from notable people in the field of giftedness and twice-exceptionality. An outside perspective can have an ameliorative effect on the community which can contribute to needs for hope. Keep an eye out for workshops in your area at local gifted support centers or other gifted schools.

More than anything, take to heart the old maxim:

Be kind, for everyone is fighting a hard battle.
~Ian MacLaren

Every gifted and 2e child expresses his or her idiosyncrasies differently. Your understanding of what it means the gifted/2e designation is going to broaden and deepen when you get to know the children in your program. Behavior which you may have become accustomed to will drive other parents up the wall, and vice versa. Watch that you do not bring unhelpful judgment to the room. Gifted children and their parents are sensitive and pick up on that stuff right away, probably having experienced it before.

If parents have a problem with any aspect of the program, encourage them not to talk about it in front of their child. That child will come to school and tell everyone! Try to save them from that embarrassment by providing them with a protocol of how to bring up challenges they are having with the program. I prefer parents to email me, and if the issue cannot be worked out over email I will follow up with a scheduled phone call or meeting.

By maintaining integrity in your communication with and about the micro-school, you are also modeling healthy communication habits for your students. Imagine a future filled with gifted/2e adults who understand the value of communicating effectively and responsibly.

My colleague Melanie at Big Minds says that building a community is critical to the success of a program like this. Everyone needs to see the vision and feel included in the mission. Families will come to the micro-school with a lot of baggage from other educational experiences. Trust in educational authority has been eroded away after a litany of traumatizing experiences. It will take time for your parents to begin to trust that you have altruistic intentions. It will take time for them to realize that one bad day is not the beginning of a downward spiral. It will take time, but it will happen. With a clear mind and a clear heart, you can help. You can build a community that comes together to support the growth of our children.

Appendix A: Sample Contract #1

One Room Micro-School for Gifted & Twice-Exceptional Children Program Contract

Program Details

The One Room program is intended to be an enrichment and academic support program for homeschoolers and their families. Though teachers hold valid teaching credentials, enrolled families are aware that we are not licensed or accredited as a school. It is the responsibility of the families to legally file their child as a homeschooler, see http://www.californiahomeschool.net/how-to-homeschool/ or http://hsc.org/legal.html for options. All curriculum materials will be supplied for registered days with the exceptions of math. Families agree to provide the math curriculum of their choice for the daily math tutorials. Program Hours are 9:00 a.m. - 2:30 p.m. Extended hours may be arranged separately.

Deposit/Fees

3 day/week: $750/month
2 day/week: $530/month
1 day/week: $300/month

Students may register for 1-3 days per week. A deposit must be made equal to your monthly fees. This deposit is held as an assurance of your commitment to the program on a semester-by-semester basis. The deposit may be applied to the last month's fees providing notice is given to do so, otherwise it will be refunded within one week after the end of the last semester enrolled. Withdrawing from the program prior to the end of the semester will result in forfeiting the deposit in full. If the teacher determines that the student is not a good fit for the program and the student is asked to leave after exhausting all the interventions, the deposit will be refunded. Deposits may be rolled over between school years.

After enrolling for a specific number of days per week for a given semester, the number may not be reduced without forfeiting a prorated portion of the deposit equal to the reduction of days. Days may be increased, however, with a corresponding increase in deposit.

If a deposit is made for our first semester (starting [month, day, year]) and our program does not have the minimum number of enrollees (3/day) by [month, day, year] deposits will be refunded in full by [month, day, year].

Monthly payments must be made by the 1ˢᵗ 5 days of the month or a $20 late fee per day will be applied. A delinquent account in excess of 7 days, without prior arrangement, is grounds to withdraw the student from the program with a loss of the full deposit.

All payments, except for deposits, will be made directly to _____.

The last week in August and the two in June will be prorated. All other months are paid in full regardless of vacation days (yours or the program's).

Child's Name/Information

Last: _____   First: _____

Grade Level: _____

Date of Birth: _____/_____/_____

Gender: M   F   Other

Previous school: _____

Address: _____

_____

Registration Period: _____Fall 2013 _____Winter & Spring 2013

Number of days per week (circle your choice): 1   2   3

Preferred Days (circle your choice): Tu Th Fr

All legally responsible parents/guardians must sign this contract showing agreement to the program and financial terms:

Signature #1: _____

Phone: _____

Email: _____

Signature #2: _____

Phone: _____

Email: _____

Accepted on (Date): _____

By: _____

Emergency Contact Information

Child's Name: _____

Age: _____

Primary Contact

Name: _____

Email: _____

Home Phone: _____

Work Phone: _____

Cell Phone: _____

Address: _____

_____

Secondary Contact

Name: _____

Email: _____

Home Phone: _____

Work Phone: _____

Cell Phone: _____

Address: _____

_____

Medical Contacts

Doctor: _____

Phone: _____

Address: _____

_____

Insurance Carrier & Policy #: _____

Dentist: _____

Phone: _____

Address: _____

_____

Insurance Carrier & Policy #: _____

Medical Information

Known allergies: _____

Current medications: _____

Other health issues: _____

Appendix B: Sample Contract #2

Big Minds Contract
2015/2016 Academic Year

Parents, guardians, or other persons responsible for payments should read all the provisions of this Contract, complete the required information, sign and return the Contract to Melanie Hayes. A student is accepted for enrollment when the Contract has been delivered to Big Minds, signed by the student's parent/guardian/responsible person and dated, and the non-refundable tuition payment has been paid in full. No amendment to this Contract and no alteration or addition to the printed terms hereof will be effective without the express prior written approval of both parties.

Student's Name: _____

Start Date:_____

In consideration of the acceptance of this Contract by Big Minds, the undersigned agrees to pay the required TOTAL TUITION for the full academic year, beginning in September and ending in June of each academic school year, payable as set forth below. So long as tuition payments are not delinquent, students are enrolled at Big Minds. Tuition payments are due on the first day of each month of the school year.

Enrollment is conditional upon the following terms:

1.   For currently enrolled students, the successful completion of the current academic year and recommendation to continue at Big Minds is required for re-enrollment.

2.   The first three month's tuition of $6,000.00 is due upon enrollment and is non-refundable. Thereafter, tuition payments must be received by Melanie Hayes on or before the first day of each month. Tuition is $2,000.00 per month. A one-time annual materials fee of $500.00 is also due upon enrollment.

3.   Acceptance of enrollment constitutes an agreement to pay the full academic year's tuition.

4.   Per state regulations, all enrolling students must show proof of immunization for: diphtheria, haemophilus influenzae type b, measles, mumps and pertussis (except for students who have reached 7 years), poliomyelitis, rubella, tetanus and any other disease deemed appropriate by the State Department of Health Services. Calif. Health and Safety Code §120325.

5.   In any action to enforce the terms of this agreement, the prevailing party shall be entitled to reasonable attorney's fees.

6.   The student and the student's family agree to comply with and are subject to the Big Mind's rules and policies as set forth in the Big Minds Contract, as amended from time to time.

7.   An account is considered delinquent if not paid within 5 business days of the due date. A late payment fee of 1-1/2% per month, or fraction of a month, will be charged on a delinquent account. Whenever a tuition or fee account becomes past due for a period of 5 days from its due date, then the student will be excluded from the premises until the delinquency is cured. If the delinquency is not cured within an additional 30-day period, the student will be dismissed. In all events, the first tuition installment of $6,000.00 must be paid on or before the first day of school or the student's place will not be reserved and the student will not be enrolled at Big Minds.

A fee of $100.00 will be charged for all checks returned for insufficient funds. Upon a second occurrence of an insufficient funds check, all subsequent payments must be made in cash.

8.   Tuition is not reduced for time away from school. The full monthly tuition is due regardless of days student has missed due to illness or vacation.

9.   It is the parents' responsibility to ensure that children are not dropped off before 8:30 a.m. and are picked up by 3:30 p.m. If you drop your child off before 8:30 a.m., or if you do not pick up your child by 3:30 p.m., alternate arrangements must be made. An additional charge of $30.00 per half hour, or portion thereof, will be added to the monthly tuition bill for students who are dropped off before 8:30 a.m. and/or not picked up by 3:30 p.m.

10. Big Minds reserves the right to terminate enrollment at any time if it is determined that: Big Minds cannot effectively meet the needs of your child; your child is a danger to himself/herself or to others; your child damages property; or your child disturbs or disrupts other students or staff.

Signature 1: _____

Date: _____

Name: _____

(Parent, Guardian, or Person Responsible for Payment)

Signature 2: _____

Date: _____

Name: _____

(Parent, Guardian, or Person Responsible for Payment)

Signature 3: _____

Date: _____

Name: _____

(Parent, Guardian, or Person Responsible for Payment)

Accepted by: _____

Signature: _____

Date: _____

Dr. Melanie Hayes, Director, Big Minds

Resources

Books

Attachment-Based Teaching: Creating a Tribal Classroom (The Norton Series on the Social Neuroscience of Education), by Louis Cozolino

Gifted, Bullied, Resilient: A Brief Guide for Smart Families, by Pamela Price

If This is a Gift, Can I Send it Back?: Surviving in the Land of the Gifted and Twice Exceptional, by Jen Merrill

Living With Intensity: Understanding the Sensitivity, Excitability, and the Emotional Development of Gifted Children, Adolescents, and Adults, by Susan Daniels (Editor), Michael M. Piechowski

Making the Choice: When Typical School Doesn't Fit Your Atypical Child, Corin Barsily Goodwin and Mika Gustavson, MFT

Nonviolent Communication: A Language of Life, by Marshall B. Rosenberg

Parenting From Your Heart: Sharing the Gifts of Compassion, Connection, and Choice, by Inbal Kashtan

The Explosive Child: A New Approach for Understanding and Parenting Easily Frustrated, Chronically Inflexible Children, by Ross W. Greene PhD

The Mislabeled Child: Looking Beyond Behavior to Find the True Sources and Solutions for Children's Learning Challenges, by Brock Eide and Fernette Eide

The Underground History of American Education, by John Taylor Gatto

Ungifted: Intelligence Redefined, by Scott Barry Kaufman

Websites & Blogs

Alfie Kohn
http://www.alfiekohn.org
"Alfie Kohn writes and speaks widely on human behavior, education, and parenting. The author of fourteen books and scores of articles, he lectures at education conferences and universities as well as to parent groups and corporations. Kohn's criticisms of competition and rewards have been widely discussed and debated, and he has been described in Time magazine as 'perhaps the country's most outspoken critic of education's fixation on grades [and] test scores.'"

Big Minds Unschool
http://www.bigmindsunschool.org
"Big Minds is an attachment-based, community focused school designed to give 2e students the time and support necessary to grow into thoughtful, articulate citizens."

Bob Yamtich, MFT
http://www.bobyamtich.com
"Connecting with the Neurodiverse"

Crushing Tall Poppies
http://crushingtallpoppies.com
"[Celi] became a passionate advocate for gifted children after tiring of her battles with schools and their misunderstanding and neglect of gifted students."

Gifted Homeschoolers Forum (GHF)
http://www.giftedhomeschoolers.org
"Changing the Way the World Views Education"

Laughing at Chaos
http://laughingatchaos.com
"Where wildly different is perfectly normal"

Legal Information
http://webapps.dol.gov/elaws/whd/flsa/docs/contractors.asp

Supporting the Emotional Needs of the Gifted (SENG)
http://sengifted.org
"SENG's mission is to empower families and communities to guide gifted and talented individuals to reach their goals: intellectually, physically, emotionally, socially, and spiritually."

The Center for Nonviolent Communication
https://www.cnvc.org
"Nonviolent Communication (NVC) is based on the principles of nonviolence-the natural state of compassion when no violence is present in the heart."

Twice-exceptional Newsletter
http://www.2enewsletter.com
"For parents, educators, and other professionals helping 2e children reach their potential."

Endnotes

1.   Yehudi Meshchaninov, "The Pre-Industrial History of Public Schooling," The New American Academy, April 2012, 5, http://www.thenewamericanacademy.org/images/the-prussian-industrial-history-of-public-schooling1.pdf.

2.   Ruth Perou, Ph.D., et al, "Mental health surveillance among children—United States, 2005-2011," Centers for Disease Control and Prevention, Morbidity and Mortality Weekly Report (MMWR), May 17, 2013, http://www.cdc.gov/mmwr/preview/mmwrhtml/su6202a1.htm?s_cid=su62 02a1_w.

3.   "Twice Exceptional—Smart Kids with Learning Differences," Gifted Homeschoolers Forum, last modified November 8, 2013, http://giftedhomeschoolers.org/ghf-press/twice-exceptional-smart-kids-learning-differences/.

4.   "The Columbus Group," Gifted Development Center, http://www.gifteddevelopment.com/isad/columbus-group.

5.   Pamela Price, "Gifted, Poor and Sassy—A Guest Post by Jade Rivera," Red, White & Grew, June 12, 2014, http://redwhiteandgrew.com/2014/06/12/gifted-poor-and-sassy/.

6.   John Taylor Gatto, "Against School: How Public Education Cripples Our Kids, and Why," Harper's Magazine, September 2003, http://harpers.org/archive/2003/09/against-school/.

7.   Dr. Linda Silverman, "Characteristics of Giftedness Scale," Gifted Development Center, 1993, uploaded 2014, http://www.gifteddevelopment.com/sites/default/files/Characteristics%20o f%20Giftedness%20Scale%202014.pdf.

8.   Corin Barsily Goodwin, "Gifted Children with Learning Challenges (Twice Exceptional)," Gifted Homeschoolers Forum, December 19, 2012, http://giftedhomeschoolers.org/resources/parent-and-professional-resources/articles/2e/gifted-children-with-learning-challenges-twice-exceptional/.

9.   Sharon Lind, "Overexcitability and the Gifted," The SENG Newsletter 2001 1(1), 3-6, http://sengifted.org/archives/articles/overexcitability-and-the-gifted.

10.   Peter Gray, "Declining Student Resilience: A Serious Problem for Colleges," Psychology Today, September 22, 2015, https://www.psychologytoday.com/blog/freedom-learn/201509/declining-student-resilience-serious-problem-colleges.

11.   Edward Schlosser, "I'm a liberal professor, and my liberal students terrify me," Vox, June 3, 2015, http://www.vox.com/2015/6/3/8706323/college-professor-afraid.

12.   Brock Eide and Fernette Eide, *The Mislabeled Child: Looking Beyond Behavior to Find the True Sources and Solutions for Children's Learning Challenges,* (New York: Hachette Books, 2007).

13.   L. Edwards and P. Torcellini, "A Literature Review of the Effects of Natural Light on Building Occupants," National Renewable Energies Laboratories: Technical Review, July 2002, http://www.nrel.gov/docs/fy02osti/30769.pdf.

About the Author

Jade Rivera is a GHF Ambassador, innovative educator, writer, and coach based in Oakland, California where she lives with her husband. Prior to her career in progressive education she was a chemist. In 2003 she earned a Fulbright scholarship for academic research in Thailand.

Jade may be reached via:
jadeannrivera.com
Twitter (@jadeannrivera)
Facebook (https://www.facebook.com/jade.rivera.988)

Made in the USA
Lexington, KY
17 May 2017